TREMBLING IN THE BONES

TREMBLING IN THE BONES

Poems

For Ruthie
With gratitude
and in friendship

ELEANOR SWANSON

GRp

Ghost Road Press
Denver, Colorado

27 January 2007

Library of Congress Cataloging-in-Publication Data.
Eleanor Swanson.
Trembling in the Bones.
Ghost Road Press
ISBN 0977803465 (Trade Paperback)
Library of Congress Control Number: 2006928753

Cover Photo: Coal Miners' Families
Denver Public Library Collection, Western History Collection
Bartosch, Call X-60475.

Book Design: Sonya Unrein

Ghost Road Press, Denver, Colorado
ghostroadpress.com

Grateful acknowledgment is made to *Nimrod International Journal*, where "Breaker Boy" and "The Dolls" originally appeared. With thanks to Matthew Davis and Sonya Unrein at Ghost Road Press, to Bob Cooperman for his comments on the manuscript, and to Herman Asarnow and Chris North for their particular encouragement and support.

For Bud
and
in memory of Gwen Terp

Contents

IV. STRIKE: LUDLOW COLONY

V. AFTERMATH

TREMBLING IN THE BONES

I thought it necessary to study history, even to study it deeply, in order to obtain a clear meaning of our immediate time.

—Paul Valéry

I. THIS NEW GARDEN

ALLOTMENT

Colorado Territory 1865

Trace the history of Arapahoe,
Ute, Cheyenne across
the Southern Plains
of Colorado.

Follow sunlight caught
in rough bison hide,
and vast herds thundering
through prairies, enveloped
in the land's glittering dust.

Before another turning of the earth,
hard sunlight bleaches the bones of buffalo
carcasses white fur traders left to rot.

High fashion changed on a whim
and the traders let their forts fall to ruin.
But already Indians had long been without meat
and their bodies were hollow with hunger.

In the mountain camps, gold miners
cut timber for their campfires
until green forests no longer rippled
across the landscape.

Without trees there must be coal to burn.

The treaties that gave the Indians
this land no longer applied.
At Sand Creek, the militia came at dawn.
When they were finished, more than
one hundred were dead under the bright
morning's eye, all now deaf to the locomotives
huffing into Denver and the singing
of the meadowlarks. All forever
blind to the liquor-colored glow of coal
gas lamps along the avenues of the Queen City.

There must be enough coal.

Everywhere its seams wind deep,
honeycombs of rich, dark coal,
wealth without end.

We must have more coal
burning red as heart's blood
in every furnace, every stove,
every locomotive, every factory.

GENERAL WILLIAM JACKSON PALMER WRITES TO MARY LINCOLN MELLEN

*Founder of the Denver & Rio Grande Railway
and the city of Colorado Springs*

"Dearest one,
Don't think me a rough man because
I have fought in the field for our grand union.
The ringing of bullets and clashing of swords
is locked in the past, and our future
as man and wife lives in view
of these majestic mountains.
I shall found a city, build a railroad
and design a railroad car as luxurious
as the finest house, with hot and cold
running water and appointments
of mahogany and German silver.
Consider the name I have in mind—'Nomad.'
I hope it strikes your fancy, wife-to-be,
and suggests the adventures we will have together,
building our way through this vast wilderness,
abundant with lumber and coal.
We will secure laborers, new immigrants,
to work the railroad and the mines."

I reflect upon the loftiness of my thoughts
as the sun begins its fiery descent,
its flames soon to fan into violent
color as it drops behind Grand Peak.
I am a man fully in control of my destiny, elevated
by this splendid light, aware that my purpose
is to civilize this land, no matter the cost.

RALPH WALDO EMERSON TRAVELS WEST
ON THE TRANSCONTINENTAL RAILROAD
1871

He looks out the window at the passing landscape
and dabs his mouth with a linen napkin.
Dinner was sumptuous, the car—named the "Huron"—
stocked by Pullman himself with fine
food and drink, delights for each
of the senses, tonics for the imagination,
as is traveling on this locomotive,
on tracks carving through the wild West.

He takes out his pen and begins
to compose a letter to his wife.
If only she could see the mountains
and plains flowing by, in rivulets
of color, so much land, all
for the taking. "My beloved
wife," he begins, never having
felt quite so sated and pleased,

"I watch a wild land stream past,
feeling the awe and terror that lies
over this new garden, all empty
of any adequate people."
Delight fills him, as well,
at the sublime thought
that God has given man
eternal charge over Nature.

MOTHER JONES VISITS COLORADO IN DISGUISE
1903

Not long before a strike was called, I disguised
myself as a peddler, and went down to the southern
coalfields of the Colorado Fuel and Iron Company.

I put on a calico dress, faded and gauzy,
such as a homely old woman would wear
as she eked out a living in the squalid coal camps.

I hid my face with a big sunbonnet, and made
my way into the windswept canyons of the Black
Hills, and to the coal towns of Tabasco and Berwin.

Mouths to the narrow canyons are guarded,
but I was allowed to pass, so meager was my attire.
I peered from beneath the brim of my bonnet

at the shoddy company cabins
perched among sandstone rocks
and thick stands of juniper.

I offered the simple sundries most
were too poor to buy, the diggers paid
only in scrip—pins, needles, elastic

and such, for making or mending clothes.
At each camp, some family would ask me
to take a meal with them and stay

the night, more often than not, bedded
down on a quilt among the children,
who wanted to touch my long white hair.

When I let it down, they stroked it,
and begged for a packet of pins
or buttons, holding out small hands.

As always, although nearly forty
years have passed since I lost them,
I could not help but think

of my own four babies, dead
of yellow fever, one by one, my
husband passing of the same sickness.

A boy reached out to me with cut palms
and fingers, a breaker boy of ten
or so who sifted rocks from coal

all day in near darkness.
I pitied him his lost childhood
and gave him a packet of my best

brass buttons, shiny as little suns.
Poor lad. I told him he must
go to school and learn to read.

He laughed. "Next I'll be a trapper
and then take up the pick," he said,
a thin child with coal-dark hair.

Enough, I thought, a word I've
thought and said ten thousand times.
Their souls slowly drift away.

Men, women and children,
all living as if they have already
been taken by the earth and its long silences.

THROUGH A GLASS, DARKLY

Near Trinidad, Colorado, 1903

She folds her hands under her head
and dreams of swallowing yellow water
that she spits at a mine guard like a snake.

When she runs away, someone hides her
in recumbent shadows, until the Purgatoire
River swallows the moon, and she floats
above it, deaf to the murmurs of the dead
struggling their way to shore.

In their dark cabin, she wakes to the cry
of a white owl long before her mother stirs.
When she's sent out for water, she twists
her dress in her hands and thinks
of the men and boys who prowl
the canyon, looking for work
in the mine that killed them.

When the shadows are fainter,
she sees that someone has thrown
a dog into the arroyo, where
it lies on a bed of straw and manure
from the mules' stables.
Its fur is still shiny-black.
Maybe it is sleeping.
She whistles, but it doesn't move.
She walks past the slack pile
and the coal ovens, wishing
she could hold her nose, but
both her hands carry buckets.

She walks past the dump, its edges
decorated with stove ashes and jars
and broken glass shining in the first sun.
She puts down the buckets and tries
to find a pretty blue piece
to take down to the creek.
She will hold it in front of her,
as if it is a big eye
that will help her see the dead,
before her hands break the surface
of the dark water.

EXPLOSION: GARFIELD COUNTY COLORADO, 1903

Olive Lawson Speaks

I'd just put Fern in her cradle,
when the back of our house exploded
and burst into flames, smoke billowing
through the rooms like almighty waves,
threshed gray, rolling past me in a silence
profound as a long sojourn under water.

I thought I was already dead, but I picked up
the baby, wrapped my shawl around her
and ran for the door, my mouth gulping air,
my throat raw, windows shattering
like sprays of diamonds, without a sound.
I nearly fell from the porch into John's arms.
Just home, he pulled us away from the burning
house, his lips moving as we ran, past
the viburnum, his mouth forming words
all the while and me hearing nothing,
not even the sound of my own sobbing.

I smelled the smoke and watched clouds
drift idly through a row of tall poplars,
weaving their way among the branches
in that silence, longer than spilled starlight.

Though John held me in his arms
and Fern's face was splotchy from crying,
I thought I was dead, but I was only temporarily
deafened from the blast that had leveled our house.

Sometimes I dream of that day—
the flames streaming towards me
like long, red petals, trying
to catch up with me and the baby,
as if we'd gone straight to hell,
though God knows we deserved better

for our part in the life of a man
who could call a strike,
stand his own in a boxing ring,
or comfort a miner's widow
with a minister's grace.

STARKVILLE MINE EXPLOSION

October 1909

The wings of the angel of death flap in the dark.
The newly widowed and fatherless hear
that whoosh overhead, the disturbed air,
the whispers of those who have come
to take out the bodies.

A makeshift morgue is prepared. "With gunny sacks
spread upon the greasy floor, and with tubs
and tables ready, the coroner waits," writes
Damon Runyon for a Denver paper.
But he can't come near the blown-out mine.
The timbers that flew out the entrance
from the force of the blast
form an enigmatic pattern.

Someone on top of Fisher's Peak could stand
under the relentless beating wings and see those
fractured beams fanning out from the mouth
of the sepulcher in the very shape of the dark angel.

The bodies will be taken out in darkness, order
the mine officials from their private rail car, beautifully
named *Sunrise*, the bodies whose terrible wounds
can't be seen for fear of panic and riots.
Reporters must stay a quarter mile away.
Orders must be followed or they'll have
their cameras smashed to bits.

Four days have passed since the blast,
and forty men and boys are finally taken out,
their dinner buckets empty, and not a mark or blemish
on a one of them, all suffocated in the afterdamp.
Like the men of Hartley Colliery, they trembled
at the end, listened in the dark to the trembling
earth and felt the air grow thin and scarce
as the coal-dark form quivered overhead, waiting.

MARY BELL HEARS THE VERDICT

That morning when I walked into the courthouse
with the other widows, I looked up at the building,
towering above the town, tall columns lining
the fronts of every floor, like a monument to a god.
Inside the courtroom sat mostly women and children.
The men had gone back to the mine just days after the blast.

My own little ones were with the woman who ran
the boardinghouse—a room there, our new home.
Without a miner husband, I'd no more rights
to our company house, meager as it was.
When I finally saw him, days after he'd died,
he looked as though he'd just lain down
for a short rest, though he'd been
smothered by the explosion's poison gas.
Not so bad in the end
as dying of a crushing wound.

Morning sun streamed through the courtroom's
stained glass windows, each with a design
of blue and gold, a red torch at the center.
What did it mean to show, I wondered?
Was it some symbol of law, or what
went on in courts? The more I stared,
the more I thought only of warmth,
each little lamp fueled by hard-gotten coal.

I held back tears and listened to the voices
of the judge and lawyers—two of the three
owned by the company.
I felt sorry for the woman next to me,
just a girl, really, whose English wasn't good.
I took her hand and nodded, as if to tell
us both this once against the odds
we'd get a proper settlement.

In a voice that droned like a bottlefly,
the company lawyer started reading,
"*...known facts of the explosion show*
the company spent thousands on ventilation...
men disregard these strict rules for safety."
Behind me, a woman started to sob,
the first, perhaps, to understand
that the verdict was already in,
and each of us whose husbands
still lay in the morgue
would walk away
with nothing.

II. WHERE THE SUN NEVER SHINES

ROBERT MARTINEZ

Victor-American mine explosion, February 1909

I went to work in the Bernal mine
when I was twelve and still wishing
on stars trailing fire, burning
through the blue-black Colorado sky,
a boy outside a cabin smelling
pinesap and wood smoke and figuring
out what I could wish for when
the next star fell, and then another.
But inside the mine, crawling on your knees
with your pick to get at the foot of the vein,
isn't like being in the night's sweet dark.

The first time I followed
my father into the ground, lucky
I wasn't just a breaker boy,
but still afraid, I watched the lamp
on my cap cast wavering shadows
on the walls and seams, like wraiths
in a nightmare or specters floating
over fresh grave sod.

As a boy, I stood upright, walking
down the long stone corridor.
As a man, I stooped as I shored
the beams and chipped coal
from the seams running along
the walls like inky rivers.
Each day, I smelled the bitter-dry
air for gas and coal dust,
and swore my own sons
would never work
in the mines.

But before I became a father,
I died with eighty other men
in the Delagua blast.

THOMAS SUTTON

Sometimes I hear water singing under the earth,
beyond the seams of coal, deep in the rock,
a soft sound, like the humming of a girl at work.
Before I left the company school to lay down tracks
in the hole, my teacher pointed, past the schoolhouse,
her arm straight as the shadow of a bird flying true north.

"Mountains," she said, "lie beyond the mine. *Huajatolla*,
breasts of the earth, twin peaks the Indians named."
Even if it takes all night, someday, after I come up
into the last light, I'll walk in that direction
and follow the road leading out
of the valley with its slag heaps and dust.

I'll climb without stopping, into clear
thin air, until I reach the Huajatolla and see
them for myself, silhouetted against the sky.
After she told us about the canaries
men used to take with them into the mine,
I never saw her again.
Even children spy for the bosses.

Once, at dusk, I saw a mountain
bluebird perched in a tall pine.
I thought of the canaries in the dark,
in their wooden cages, tasting the stale
air while the miners watched
their every breath, listened to each note
they trilled, waiting to hear the sound
of blood and bones in their faint songs.

SPACE AND THE DARKNESS BEYOND

Six days a week he goes down, fourteen hours
a day, down with the other miners to chip
at seams of bitter-black coal, loading
the car to send what he's mined to the surface.
If he was an artist he'd carve
the coal into vicious black dolls
he could pray to or burn
as sacrifices to the disemboweled Mother.

He'd see the traces of ancient
worlds on the coal's shining surface,
diatoms and curling tips
of ferns frozen in an inky sea.
He'd paint chaos, boldly
laying black upon black
or sketch the cretaceous
landscape with delicate strokes.
He could have been that man,
he thinks, feeling the rock
tremble and sigh under
his trailing fingertips,
as he imagines himself called
by the tons of coal that have laid
their dark wash on his hand and arms.

He thinks of how he has run
his hands along the dark seams,
of how deep he is, how the small light
of his cap creates space and the darkness
beyond is a void.
An artist has to go deep down somewhere,
before he takes up a pen or a brush
and caresses his work with the touch of a lover.
When he goes to the heart of the earth,
he wants to find something there!
Something more than the dust
and dark stink of men and mules.
Something more.

NAKED

The man's hands are gnarled maps.
Imagine his crooked fingers
in darkness holding to the lip
of a coal car.

At night, sometime near dawn,
he clasps his wife's hands.
They are like paths
to places stranger to him

than the depths of the Aguilar mine.
He holds her fingertips
to his ear and listens
for a long time until

silence gives way
to the muffled hum
of summer bees.
She tries to straighten

her man's hand, stroking
the coarse blue-skinned
palm, expecting it to sputter
into quiet flame.

She takes the hand to her mouth
and one by one commands
each of the fingers to rest,
to sleep out the darkness.

For a while the man dreams
of playing baseball,
grasping a bat and swinging
toward pure outfield light.

He drops the bat and takes
a base, running down into
a tunnel deeper than the mine.
When once again his hands

shape themselves into instruments
of mere toil and toil alone,
he rises from the bed and
hurries to cover his naked body.

BREAKER BOY

When he was nine, he told the pit
boss he was twelve, going on
thirteen, small for his age.
At five a.m., his first morning out,
he and his father drink bitter
coffee and eat biscuits
and gravy, a taste that stays
with him thick as a mouthful
of bad words.

On the way to the breaker
he spits like a man, then climbs
the dark stairway to the screenroom,
breathing in dust and the reek
of soot he will live with
through his shift, and the next
and another until, blessedly,
he forgets altogether the wild
roses gnarling through boulders
along a rough path, giving up
their smell of spice and sun.

The bench where he sits
all day lies across an iron chute
chunks of coal rumble through.
His job is simple—pick out
the rock and slate.
He makes a game of being
quick with his fingers.

At night his mother draws
his hands into hers and tends
his cuts with stinging iodine.
He thinks, next I will go
into the mines and be a door
boy, opening and shutting,

letting the men and cars in
and out and learning to whistle
"Sally Ann" while I whittle
wood dolls for my sister
with troll faces and long
sharp teeth, like the ones
on all those rocks.

TREMBLING IN THE BONES

There's not a man or boy who hasn't sensed
what few underground can always name—
a feeling you're inside something
with its own being, neither human or animal,
but nonetheless alive, breath rank,
full of damp cavities and chambers,
dark blood hissing invisibly
along the whole length of it.

When the trembling in its bones begins,
set up by the creature's slightest shift
or shudder, it crosses into your own blood,
sets your own bones to trembling
and stuns you with fear you'll be taking
your last breath in a pure-dark seam.

At the New Hartley Colliery,
after the engine that powered
the cages broke and tumbled into
the shaft, blocking their only exit,
two hundred and four men and boys—
most of the men of the town—listened,
gave up their lights
and lay quietly, sipping
the waning air.

They spent their final hours praying,
talking softly among themselves
and writing goodbyes to mothers, fathers,
wives and sweethearts, a few
words they wanted to leave behind.
Mercy, O God!
Goodbye Mother, Love, Tom.
With a nail, a hewer scratched
words on a shot box: *Friday*
afternoon, My dear
Sarah, I leave you.

They leaned on their elbows
in the mine gallery, breathing
their last shallow breaths
and listening to the great body
invaded by dying men
trembling in the bones.
Rescuers found them side-by-side,
sons' hands
on fathers' shoulders, brothers
embracing, as if they merely slept
after a long day's work.

III. YOUNG BLOOD MAKES A HOT FIRE

GLENDA DOWNIE LISTENS

Lying sleepless beside my husband,
I listen to the sounds of midnight,
light, complicated noises,
like an embroidery on a dark
cloth fine as air itself.
My husband snores softly and frets,
rolling this way and that, then settles.
Outside, wind shudders through pines,
muffling a hoot owl's cries.
I've always had good ears
and used them many a time
to seek out solitude amid
the maddening noise of everyday,
or as a way to learn secrets
and enter into mysteries
beyond the ken of most.

Keen hearing's almost better
than the gift of prophecy.
That's a footstep now, a boot
crushing a twig, and another.
Strangers in the camp
who've gotten past the guards.
My ears tell me more
than my mind knows.
It's union men come to organize
this near-beaten band of men
and boys, into a boisterous force
that the bosses will finally hear,
voices roaring like rushing water
sweeping over the land.

ILIAS ANASTASIOS SPANTIDAKIS WRITES
TO HIS MOTHER IN CRETE

"Dearest One,"
I begin the letter to my mother,
"I have left the Market Street
coffee shop in Denver for steady work
in the coal fields of southern Colorado."

I don't tell her I started as a scab
in the northern fields
and found myself no more
than a slave, making thirty-nine
and a half cents a ton.
I led a walkout, then went
down into the southern
fields to organize.

"I still have the packet of Greek
earth you sewed into the seam
of my good shirt," I write.
I find the words to tell her
I am all right, I am well.

"You wouldn't have believed
how the men in the shop broke
out into the songs of the great
grandfathers as if they wanted
to hear the crackle of guns
and taste the blood from
those days of long ago."

At this her eyes will mist over.
"Young blood makes a hot fire,"
I imagine her whispering.
I plan an answer in my words.
"Don't worry, my dearest mother.
I will do nothing rash,
but will be brave at all I do."

I think of the time I have already
spent in prison, and recite
a proverb of my own—I live too near
the woods to be scared by owls.
"Here in America, I go by
Louis Tikas, though sometimes
they call me Louie the Greek."

Soon we will sling bandoliers
across our shoulders,
and knot red bandannas around
our necks, the strikers' emblem.
"Please go to a letter writer
in Rethymnon and send me
some word of yourself
and of our family and friends
in Lautra, my beloved village.
Love to you always,
my dearest mother."

HOUSE OF ICE

A year ago in spring, as I clutched at the scented
air that trailed him like a second self,
my husband left our village near Calabria.
When he sent for me, I followed,
enduring rough water—a plain of ocean
carved into whitecaps, my heart
pulsing fear, all those weeks at sea,
and on to "processing" at Ellis Island,
the first new English word I learned,
those harsh letters filling my head
like the cry of a scolding bird.

On the train to Trinidad, Colorado,
I hold my papers on my lap, everything
I need for the new land under my hands.
At night, in dreams, the papers tremble,
then take the shape of *saturos*
who dance around my ankles
chanting in Sicilian, "Without us
you have nothing."
I know the feeling of having less
than nothing, and am afraid.

When the sun comes up and fills the car
with light, I show my papers when I'm asked
though I want to cry "I don't like it here!"
Non mi piace. I don't like it.
But I tell myself what I need to know—
I am Carlotta, I am eighteen, I am strong.
My husband is a pick man in the mine.
I watch the gathering clouds, then rain,
then windows streaked and blurred with white.
I step off the train into fierce wind, looking
down the platform for my Vincente.

Sleet burns my face as Vincente takes me
to Delagua Canyon in an open cart,
to our company house where the rough
coal they have given him won't burn.
I sleep that night beneath my mother's
quilts in this place, no more
than a shack, my new house of ice.

VEIL OF COAL DUST

The land wears the veil always, worse
to see it on snow, from inside,
where my elbows wear a froth
of soapy water, like tattered lace.

I take my hands from the water
and look at them palms up—
fat, red hands, nicked and scarred
from cooking, cleaning, laundry,
fetching water for every chore,
waiting for the babies
to sleep so I can work for once
without their tears or shrieking play.

My hands. I smooth down my apron
and give them a minute
to be still, for each to dream
its own fine dream.

Back in the last coal town
I had boarders to feed and clean
up after, more money, too,
a little garden of vegetables,
chickens and a milk cow.

By spring I'll find ground
under the ashes good
for planting and take in some
bachelor Italians, and for now
hush Jack when he has nightmares
of a roof fall or river of fire.
I'll scrub the coal dust
from the floors and walls,
and tell him what I've learned
from the silence, when
the children are sleeping—

that silence has a taste,
sweet as melon.

I'll tell him what I've learned
from my own dancing,
dreaming fingers—
that they each wear

satin and veils
of silk and are made
for more than work.

MARGUERITE MCCONNELL

Hastings Camp, 1913

As he drinks scalding coffee from a tin cup,
I ask my husband what it's like
to ride the cage down to the shaft.
A few grounds cling to his mustache.
I want to reach up and brush them away,
but I don't dare, lest I make him think
of the warm bed, his arms around me,
our bodies entwined, the morning
so fresh upon us.

His mind is focused on the rocky path
he takes to the mine's mouth
with other men and boys, a careless line,
snaking through predawn dark.
I think he hasn't heard my question.
He doesn't look my way as he pulls
on his overalls, black in the folds
despite washboard scrubbings.
But his voice comes soft as if he's
spoken from beneath the pit itself.
"My dear girl," he says, "My good
Marguerite. Why do you ask?
But listen. You've heard its depths
in many a mournful fiddle tune
I've played through a late night.
Listen for the darkness,
the danger in every note.
Note by frenzied note I've spun
the only tales I'll ever tell
about that damp, winding road
down to hell.

They say it runs in the blood,"
he says with a laugh that cleaves
the air, "but there's no good in slaving,
in the pit, save what our imagination
grants us, of the sweet love of wives
and their touch, or of the whisperings
of a strike to come. Listen, my dear."

VALLEY OF ASHES

The morning light is frail as the stalk
of a lily, greenish, as if ready to droop
back into night and put out the sun.
I've traveled all the way from my lush
valley in Wales, a miner's daughter
and now a miner's wife, staring out
the doorway at desolation, not a tree
or anything green as far as I can see,
only rows of unpainted shacks, just
a step between front stoop and dusty,
dirt street, gray as a layer of ashes
in the feeble dawn.

Back home, our company bungalows
were built of native stone, our valley
ringed by mountains, wildflowers
dotting the green meadow grass
with a hundred colors.

As I watch the woman across the road
scrub clothes on a big washboard,
I begin to cry.
My two little girls are asleep, oblivious
to the dirty light, the stretch of gray streets
that will flow with mud in the spring.
They don't yet hear the mine's
machinery grating out the minutes,
or the sound of cloth rubbed vigorously
against corrugated metal.
When they awake, I'll plait their hair
without ribbons and dress them in gray,
as I begin to teach them to live without color.
I will teach them not to miss trees,
tender grass or flowers.

They will learn to love their gray dresses
and the landscape of dirt, rock and brush.
They will learn to see beauty
in a diatom on a lump of coal,
or a dust phantasm
rising in a sudden wind.

LULLABY: EMMA STAVRIANOS SINGS TO HELEN

Don't cry, sweet Helen. I'll stoke the fire,
rock you in my arms and sing a song
about our village, the rocks, the sun, the gods
and goddesses who knew Crete as their home
and intervened for mortals who suffered
far beyond their due, like your father here
who's lost the sun, forgotten the sea's shine,
its blue sweep, the silvery olive trees.

Perhaps he sometimes dreams of home
and then in sleep forgets awhile
the dark labyrinth of the mine and imagines
himself *palikari*, hero, who like Diogenes
every day wrestles death.

My sweet baby girl, we must live bravely
among the other brave women and men
here in the snow-swept canyons
so far from our homes.

La, la. I will tell you about
the White Mountains of Crete.
Oh, let time stop for a while
so that our fleeting lives might be
measured in songs and celebrations
of the glory of each season,
and not by coal cars rolling
along the tracks and the shriek
of the mine whistle.

La, la. Sleep, sleep sweetly now.
We will live bravely
until we can finally leave
this wretched place.

BILLY IN THE LOWGROUND

Inside Tabasco camp it's Saturday night
and the miners' wives string up paper
lanterns just as the bats begin to flap
in arcs in the blue milk of twilight,
making their strange, high-pitched
squeals before they disappear
into the black junipers.

The miners' dance band features
Marco on the fiddle, who strikes up
"Billy in the Lowground," a tune
about a man who falls in a deep
hole, and plays his fiddle till
folks gather round to save him.

Marco's fiddle kindles fire in the band
and dancers. He's Billy, and playing
for Billy, who's like the miners down
in the hole, where they watch
the big, keen-eared rats who hear
the timber shifting before any man
and scurry up the shaft to light.

Blending in the crowd, among the dancers,
some dancing themselves, are organizers
recruiting for the union right under the noses
of the Baldwin-Felts detectives.

Following a rat's no way to keep a man
safe from being crushed by a falling pillar,
or from suffocating in a blocked chamber.

The union men whisper among
the miners about bringing men together
for the cause—fair pay for work,
a safe pit and more.

Dancers begin to pass their partners
hand to hand, "around the world,"
it's called, dancing under the arms
of other dancers in a line that begins
to coil ever more tightly into a spiral,
woven strong, that only the dancers
themselves can break.

STRIKE CALL

Mother Jones speaks at the Trinidad Opera House

Every day, it's been in the news, "Angel
of the coal camps on her way to Trinidad."
Today, the streets are alive, me parading
behind a brass band with other miners,
weightless in sunlight, no tools, no Davy caps.

Taking a place in line at the Opera House,
I wait and listen to the talk around me,
those who've seen Mother Jones, those
who haven't, all with stories of how she shared
a prison cell with rats as big as our own
mine rats, and bid a group of miners' wives
armed with sticks and brooms break up
a scab camp down canyon.

I'm near the front of the line.
Mike Sekoria, a Slav, fired for organizing
within earshot of a spy, motions to me
and points to a saloon. I shake my head.
I'll keep my place, see and hear what I've
come for, night falling now, soft as water
flowing down a hillside, gas streetlamps
hissing into muted light and color.
I smell the autumn air, could swear
I hear the rustle of leaves turning.

When the line begins to move, thousands
behind me, I can't believe no one jostles,
everybody getting along, fine as silk.
My seat is in the second row, near center.
The house lights dim, and then rise again.
A little white-haired lady in a black dress
steps on stage, and applause starts up,
like an explosion, whistling, shouting,
going on and on, even as she walks

towards us, drawing long pins from
her hat and throwing them out for us
to catch, all of us reaching toward her,
most grasping only air, but when I open
my hand, I hold a pin, topped with a white pearl.
I stick it in my coat's lapel, and clap
and clap, as she lets down her long white hair,
straightens her shawl, then puts up her hand,
commanding silence.

She begins to speak and pace the stage,
her voice low and strong as she cusses
Rockefeller and Colorado Fuel and Iron,
and then commands us to stand up for ourselves.
"They don't think you're as valuable as their mules.
Get backbone, stick together, and fight.
And if you're afraid to fight, we'll get
the women to fight for you, and beat
the hell out of the mine owners."

She waves her hands in the air. "I say
strike!" each word piercing us like needles.
People clap and roar, shouting agreement.
"The banner of freedom will wave
over every coal mine in the state of Colorado."

When she finishes, the house echoes once again
with roaring applause and foot-stomping.
Two hours have passed as if ten minutes, and I sit
watching the spot where she'd stood.
People file out until I am alone, still watching,
as if waiting for her to reappear, and tell me
I'll never be a slave again.

I take the hatpin, prick my finger, draw blood
and sign my name on the cement floor
to say, *I am here, I have been here.*
I will strike.

DAN MACGREGOR RECOUNTS THE MINERS' EXODUS

Writing for the *Denver Express*,
I tried to describe what I saw
that morning, calling the striking miners'
struggle down the canyon roads an "exodus of woe,"
thousands of people born to suffering
going forth to more suffering.

Years later, I still remember the day—September 23, 1913.
Their forced flight from the coal camps started at dawn,
in muddy light. Thick clouds shrouded the sun
and rain mixed with snow had begun to fall.
In the cold and biting wind, I could barely feel
my fingers as I wrote about the endless stream
of wagons and pushcarts filled with meager
belongings—broken furniture, piles of straw
bedding, crockery and cookware.
I watched the armed guards swagger
from house to house, shouting insults—
Get out! You damn foreigners, get out!
Those without carts or wagons soon found
themselves and everything they had
on the muddy streets, where they sat
drenched by the freezing rain.
The intermingled sound of the guards'
curses and the cries of women and babies
pierced the air, as if it were a cloth
being rent to tatters, drifting in shreds.
Sometimes over the course of that miserable
day, I'd hear a woman singing a song
of the old country to her children,
and her man, too, to try to calm them.

Sleepless that night in my hotel,
with the sound of wind,
the wails of infants, and those songs
circling round and round in my head,

I wondered what would become of them.
I saw their faces in a cavalcade, Swedes
and Slavs, Italians, Negroes, Mexicans
and more. A thousand faces stitched
themselves into my memory—
anguished faces that said
they had suffered worse in the mines,
at the hands of a guard, or in the company store.

Walking out of the squalid camps
was a triumph for those broken souls.
But I was merely watching and taking notes.
What did I know? Each successive word
stabbed me with guilt, that I was not among them.
I vowed to fight for them, *with* them, no matter the risk.
Sometimes words are not enough.

ALICE LOWE TELLS GIRLIE ABOUT THE STRIKE

My daughter's just a small child, but quick
of mind, tender as the prairie's first green,
apt to be tearful at the smallest creature's pain.
From our nearby farm she watched, elbows
on the window sill, and when she turned
to look at me, her eyes seemed to hold
the images of what she'd seen, a long
procession coming down the canyon
in the rain, then sleet—unseen babies
screaming, dogs with drenched fur
creeping alongside rickety carts.
She never asked; her silence became
a daylong question, the day endless
with her silence, the songs she sang
to the chickens while we looked
for eggs full of nonsense words,
and I all the while wanting to weep
as the day grew shadows and the mud
grew thicker, deeper and the line
seemed never to end.

When the tents came, white canvas
set in grids, streets with names,
row upon row, and the rains
stopped, she asked. "Why
are the people living there, Momma?
Where are their real houses?"
The room grew quiet and quieter
as I thought of how to tell her.
If only her father, a railroad man
in sympathy with the striking miners
were here to describe what it meant
to crowd into a cage and go down
the black shaft to timber and shore
for not even a dime, then to dig
all day only to find at the end
the company's check weighman
cheated you on your load.

I try to find something to say.
No wonder she sang in nonsense
words that terrible day.
She waits for me to speak.
"After they went on strike,
they couldn't stay in houses
the company built."
"What is a strike?"
she asks, and I think
of how I'll answer,
knowing a long story
is about to begin.

IV. STRIKE: LUDLOW CAMP

SNOW CHILD

In the Ludlow camp, I lived in the snow,
invisible as a jackrabbit in winter, sinking
into the soft, new banks, playing
with the other children in the white clots.

When the scabs poured off the train,
surrounded by guards, we thought
of our own torn skin, scraped
and rough from the cold and wild
play no mother could stop.

We thought of cuts crusted over
and blood and scars.
I was a child,

       and time was caught in a cage.

After my mother prayed the rosary,
I took her beads and buried them in snow.
Then I fell back upon them, like a dying bird

       crashing to earth.

I lay in snow, my face
to the sky, arms outstretched, moving
up and down, legs scissoring in and out,
carving a deep place for myself.

I listened for my mother's prayers.
I called other children out into the snow,
and we lay on our backs like beetles
who'd never fly again.

Freed, time walked around us on fractured feet.

We pressed our bodies into the snow
until the sun sank behind the mountains.
When we got up, shadows had pooled
in the shapes we'd carved.

The ground was covered with cups of shade.

I put my ear to the cold place my heart
had been and listened for my mother's
prayers but heard nothing
but my own wings,
still beating there, alive,
where I had left them.

GENERAL CHASE COMMANDS THE CALVARY TO RIDE DOWN THE WOMEN

I stood in the crowd with the others,
a thousand strong, women with shabby
clothes, carrying babies and I, a girl
of fifteen with yellow hair that shone
in the afternoon sun, a quick laugh,
and a rage that sometimes spun through me
head to toe as though I'd swallowed a whirlwind.
Why did we live like rats in a sewer?
Why did they arrest Mother Jones?
They took away our banner: "Has Gov.
Ammons forgot he has a mother?"
We marched up Commercial Street,
then tuned east on Main.
Near the Post Office, the Calvary blocked
our path, sabers drawn and gleaming.
I laughed! I laughed and headed
for the edge of the crowd, where General
Chase wheeled his horse from side to side
before the front rank, yelling "Turn back!"
in the harsh voice of someone used
to giving men orders to kill other men.
But we never thought of stopping, a crowd
two counties strong marching for our fathers
and brothers and sons—and for ourselves.

When I reached the edge of the pavement,
I watched that pretty horse, with a hide
smooth and shiny as satin cloth
eyes wide and black and ears pricked
up with startlement and fear.
I watched the horse prancing toward us,
the General's feet swinging
in the stirrups, him yelling all the while
and coming closer as we kept walking,
until his spurred foot struck a girl
in the chest, setting his horse off-balance

It stumbled and reared up
and the General slipped off
and fell to the cobblestones
in a heap of dirtied uniform
and braid. Being nearby, I
was the first to laugh and then
the laughter and the jeers rippled
through the whole crowd.

When Chase remounted, he pulled
out a pistol and waved it furiously
in the air, his voice bellowing out
to the men in his command—
"Ride down the women!"
As they tore flags from our hands,
we fought them off with signs and banners,
fought off those flashing sabers,
their blades like waves of fire,
and sabers meeting hands spread
across faces, meeting foreheads and ears,
drawing bright streams of blood.
One girl had her toes smashed by a rifle butt.

I could tell you more, just from
what I read later in the papers,
how women's screams echoed
up and down Main Street,
how women and children ran
in all directions, but, in truth,
my memories froze, when that stock
came down on my foot,
the pain of the blow and its phantom
echoes, lasting now more than
half a lifetime.

PHOTOGRAPH OF MEN, WOMEN AND CHILDREN AT LUDLOW COLONY

"For a second's more sunlight men must fight like tigers."
Mother Jones

Before the strike I set up a five-by-seven
view camera at the portal of a mine
and waited for the shift's end
when men with black faces trailed
from the hole, picks on their shoulders,
lard buckets in their hands, still wearing
their caps, lights extinguished as they rose,
squinting at the sun's last ferocious fire.

After the strike began, deep into winter,
I prowled the tent colony, waiting for a chance
to frame an image of men idle, women
behind those canvas walls washing,
cleaning, patching, hoarding, scrimping,
traveling on the muddy path between
wash line and coal pile, children
with homemade toys, the white landscape
a strange vast playground, and Lou Dold
looking through the camera's big eye,
the world upside down, me watching
all of them, watching them waiting
for the decent thing to be done,
waiting for new dress, a small rabbit
for the pot, lace curtains fluttering
in a real window with shiny glass panes.

Two boys called to me to take their picture,
boys in matching overalls, dark shirts,
caps pulled low on their foreheads,
brothers dressed as twins.
I stood them in front of a tent,
just as a young woman peered out
then in a moment came
to stand next to the boys.

"Wait," she said in accented English.
The woman went in the tent again,
and came out, trailed by two little
girls, bows freshly tied in their hair;
she was carrying a baby swaddled
in a blanket. An older woman stepped
out to stand behind her and then another,
both draped in their Old World shawls.
Men from nearby tents approached
from all directions, smoking cigarettes
and pipes, and a woman who looked like
she'd just put on a clean, starched apron
joined the group and clasped her hands,
waiting to be posed.
She smiled. More joined the group
until fourteen souls in all, stood in front
of tent number eighty, looking with great
intensity straight into my camera—
the men, women and children of the Ludlow Colony,
all waiting for me to take their picture.
Waiting. Not even breathing.
I took a breath myself of the pure,
raw air, held it, and released the shutter,
as if that simple movement
could both capture and free them.

CHARLIE COSTA PLAYS A JOKE

With a stick, I draw a picture in the dirt
of a train and make the sound a train makes.
"Woo woo," I call to my bare feet,
to my toes, wishing I could have
a real train or any toy.

I kick a rock past our tent, pretending
I'm playing Kick the Can,
but it hurts my foot, so I stop in front
of the Costa's tent where Mr. Costa
is pretending a circus is going on,
saying "Come one, come all,"
and motioning to the kids nearby
who like him because he makes us
laugh, even when we're hungry
and tells us to call him Charlie.

He says my name and gives
me a newspaper rolled up
like a spyglass.

He says it costs a penny
and his wife Cedi yells,
"Did you buy spyglasses
when we are starving?"
We kids yell too, "Let's see."
When he hands me my telescope,
I put it to my eye and look around
wishing I could see stars
or the moon, right now, in the day.
I look down the row of tents
for my mother.
I want to see her.
I want her to be pretty.

All of a sudden, everyone is laughing.
Charlie has put charcoal on our telescopes,
and we all have black eyes.
We are all laughing and can't stop.
Even though we are hungry,
we can't stop laughing
at our funny black eyes.

I put the spyglass up to my other eye
so I will look like a raccoon.
This time I will see things
only raccoons can see,
stars and planets just for raccoons.

STRAW JESUS RIDES A BLACK STALLION

We were the targets of his outright hatred,
we strikers and our families, the brutal
commander of the militia, Lieutenant Karl
Linderfelt, who made no effort to conceal
his loyalty to the coal company.

His story's something out of a dime western,
where he's the crazy villain, but his villainy
wasn't honed on any dusty small-town street.
We learned he'd gotten his ideas of justice
in the Philippines from burning jungle
villages and torturing prisoners
he spat on and called *nigger* or *googoo*.
We were no better than the Filipinos,
shabby, poor and impudent, men
with whom he also waged a war,
a stocky, bull-faced man who rode
through Ludlow on a black horse shouting,
"I am Jesus Christ and I must be obeyed,"
a violent fanatic no more like Jesus
than a scarecrow in a field,
but with the power of his uniform a fiend,
who once herded us up canyon, and put
us against a wall to face a firing squad.
After he ordered his riflemen to fire,
he laughed, dismissed them and freed us,
then let his men mount and chase us
back down canyon with pickaxe handles
and bullwhips, screaming insults at our backs.

Believing himself a titan, he gave
the order to open fire on the colony
and burn our tents, then murdered
our leaders, Tikas and Fyler,
violence and hatred bred into a man
Jesus himself would find
hard to love.

I am standing next to a table with other miners'
wives and we are making food for the strikers.
I am mixing cake batter in a bowl and smiling.
I study my own face, the way my arm curves
towards its mission, the way I watch
my fingers grasping a spoon
as if I see it going about its work magically.

We are a crowd, we women, working around
the table as if we have been conjured,
we foreigners from here and there
who learned the English word for "strike"
before we learned the one for "bread."
Next to me stands Maria, who taught
me how to knead a lump of dough
until its surface glistened
like a newborn's skin.

Cedi stands across from me.
She died in the cellar with her little
ones, Lucy, Onafrio, and Frank
when the militia burned our colony.
Charlie, her husband died, too,
shot in the back running to his tent
to get Cedi and their children.
As he was dying, he asked
to hear a union song.

I thank the stranger who handed
me this photograph, an image
that keeps alive the story
of who I was then
and what I learned to do,
and the memory of each
of these strong women.

MILITIA MAN

From the other side of the fence
I watch them as they go about their day,
sometimes pointing my Winchester
in the direction of a single man
and holding him in my sights
for a while, not knowing if he knows
I can see his every move.

I never think of pulling the trigger,
for the truth is, I hate guns, I hate
most of the men who stand
on this side of the fence with me,
smoking, drinking whiskey, cursing
the miners with every other breath.

I set down my gun and take in
the camp—children playing,
a few men skinning rabbits,
bedding and clothes flapping
in the March wind.
The whole valley stretches
out before me,
on a day without gunfire.

It's not to last.

I hear the fellows talking
in the barracks at night
about how they've had enough
of the "damn foreigners"
and how they're ready
to burn the camp to the ground.

I'll light the first torch myself,
says one.
I'm nineteen and I don't want
to die or kill.
I only want out of this place.
I lift my rifle and stare
into the sights, seeing the flames,
the embers like fallen stars,
the shame of Ludlow trailing
me like a tail of fire.

MINER AND WIFE: PHOTOGRAPHER UNKNOWN

One of several dozen photographs of miners, standing in front of
their houses, collected by A.R. Mitchell, a Trinidad, Colorado,
artist

I study the details of light and shadow,
thinking *chiaroscuro*, thinking how
I might magnify the details obscured.
I think of depth, darkness, my illusion
that the photograph captures them,
man and woman, standing a few
feet apart, light gathered in the woman's
white blouse, light billowing in its long
puffy sleeves, darkness in her dark
skirt brushing the ground, dark hair
swept up atop her head, arms at her sides.
Does she think she holds them stiffly?
Does the photographer gesture her
into a pose, using his hands
to tell her how to stand?

The man has stepped into the foreground,
locating himself closer to a tree
than to his wife, his expression wary,
his stance jaunty. His feet are placed
so that he's ready to spring clear
of someone in a fight, or falling timber.
He wears a battered hat. Battered?
Seen better days?
No longer shapely.
Never new.
White suspenders and a dark,
handlebar mustache, a metaphor
for control of what it means to be a man.
They both look directly into the camera.
A coal shovel leans against the house.
His pit clothes hang on the inside wall to his right.
Do I see a chair? It's very dark inside.

The house is made of small, rough timbers
ready to be plastered with adobe, a *Jacal*
house, it's called in Mexico, the man
and woman's home country.
How is a house like a home
country? I have so much to ask them.

I want the photographer, too, to tell
me, what he was thinking
when he captured this image:
Miner and Wife.
Photographer unknown.

WOMAN KNEADING DOUGH

For Cedi and Charlie Costa

As her husband leaves Ludlow Colony
to join miners staked out in the nearby
hills, he kisses her and the children,

but she doesn't put down the dough
she has been kneading; she holds it,
smooth, silky dough, like the skin

of something ready to form itself into life.
As she stares at that pale shape,
she thinks she sees herself there, a face

with a hint of a smile, because her time
in the camp, with the other women,
has been good, all those languages

they shared words in, words
for food, and the names of children—
but now her husband is going off

with a gun and telling her
not to worry, he will be back.
She kneads the dough harder.

What would she do with her
hands otherwise? Wring them
in anguish? Cover her face

with them? Use them
to wipe away her tears?
She watches her husband run,

gun in hand, until he disappears.
This dough will make good bread,
she thinks, warm, nourishing bread

for her and the children.
She will watch it rise, fire up
the cookstove and bake it,

that delicious smell helping her
remember that the striking miners,
their wives and children worked

in the colony like a family.
When the bread is done, she will break
off steaming pieces and share them |

among all the women she lives with here.
When a bullet whizzes past her, she ducks,
and hurries inside her tent to finish

what she has started.
Nothing can stop her
but death itself.

SILENT WITNESS

Monday, April 20, 1914, Ludlow Camp

Over the colony megaphone a voice repeated,
"Run!" the words echoing in my head
like the thundering of blood, a man's voice,
frantic in pitch, crackling out like flame.
Two explosions had already shattered
the morning's calm. "The third bomb
will go off soon," said the voice,
and with a child clinging to each hand,
I ran out of the tent colony,
through the low brush, prickly pear
and yucca, rough stones, half-slipping,
waiting for the blast, my whole body
listening for the sound, like a swimmer,
waiting for the mighty force of a breaking wave.
When it came, I found myself still
running in the wake of that noise,
the bullets sounding too, and the screaming.

I lost a shoe, and when I bent to put it on
again, a bullet grazed my wrist, searing
like flame, blood dripping down my hand
onto my skirt. Thank God my older
daughter ran ahead, her hair flying
in the wind like it did when she played
Needle's Eye in the camp.
But this was no game, the prairie
covered with people running
for their lives, all of our belongings
left behind in our tents, our children's
meager toys, jack straws and pin wheels,
cloth balls and dolls, my own girl's doll
left sitting on her cot, a silent witness
to the day's events and what would come next.

Oh, what she would have seen.
If only she had been able
to testify to what had transpired
that long day and night,
her painted face come to life,
her fixed mouth given words,
before they set the camp on fire,
before the flames consumed her.

MY MOTHER'S CAMEO

Margo Gorci, Ludlow Camp, April 1914

When the shooting stopped, I climbed
the arroyo's slick walls, keeping my head
low, in case the gunfire began again.
But all I could hear was my breathing
and the sighs of birds getting ready for twilight.
From time to time as I peered at the empty
camp, the woman below me moaned.
She was huge in the belly, her baby
ready to come any time amid this chaos
of flying bullets, women and children
frightened half out of their wits, striking
miners firing at the militia from the low hills.

I never realized before how beautiful
our tents were, tent after tent, side
by side, like white birds, their wings
outstretched, all resting, like me,
in the silence between bullets.
I imagined them rising, giant birds
with soft wings, rising above the fighting,
leaving the little we owned for all
to see, for the militia to loot,
if they dared, our husband's bullets
striking near their feet.
No one would find my mother's
cameo, for I had put it in a small box
and buried it beside our tent.
A bullet whined nearby
and I slipped back down with the others.
Perhaps I could make it through the night,
if I thought about that calm, ivory
face, the mouth's slight smile,
the tendrils of hair, a frozen beauty
I would never see again.

I touched the pregnant girl beside me,
who was crying now, and wondered
what she had to bequeath to the baby
who would take its first breath
on this harrowing night.
I hoped her love would be enough
for a child born to the intertwined
sounds of tears and gunfire.

MIDNIGHT, LUDLOW DEPOT

The clock strikes midnight in the Ludlow depot.
Weak light casts troubled, unsleeping faces in pallor.
My son Frank's face was calm in death,
when I tried to finish washing him,
his dire wound unseen, the heavy bullet
that tore through the back of his skull spent in earth.
Now he's wrapped in a gunny sack
and I hold him next to my heart.

Some hours ago, when the firing slackened—
carrying my small daughter in one arm
and my dead son on my back—
I ran to the station, the rest of my family
behind me, to begin our all-night wait
for the train to Trinidad.

Now we sit, five sleeping children and a sixth
who will never awaken, listening to laughter
in the next room.

How dare they, Major Hamrock's motley "soldiers,"
carry on their laughing and boasting in our hearing,
all of them so full of liquor they can hardly stand?
At the thought one of them murdered my boy,
I want to take a gun and kill them all.

But I don't own a weapon, not even arming myself
when the strike was called, caring only from the day
we pitched our tent to keep my family from all harm.
Within a week of the walkout, I'd dug a pit under
our tent, sixteen by twenty-four,
partitioned with a curtain,
our safe home, before the shooting started.
That day, when the firing died down,
Frank ran out to get us water.
I saw the bullet spin him half way
round, and knew he'd died
before he hit the earth.

Crawling through fierce
shooting, that started up again,
I tried to go to him, to clean his face,
but only had time to cross his arms
on his chest before I made my way
back to our pit.

From under the tent floor, we felt explosions
rock the ground, until the canvas was ripped open
and set on fire, and they cursed and screamed
at us to "Get out, God damn quick."

I lay my first-born on the depot floor, and hold
my wife, whose body shakes with sobs.

I'll leave to others to tell more about that night,
when, as if the hands of an almighty clock
had broken, and time would never more
move forward, we sat until the train came.
In town, we walked to MacMahon's mortuary,
where I watched a man named Dold set up
his camera and catch a final image of our Frank,
the light of the magnesium flash burning
for an instant like holy fire,

if there is anything left that is holy in this world.

ANASTASIOS SPANTIDAKAS LEARNS OF THE DEATH OF HIS SON, ILIAS

Child of my old age, you traveled to America
when you were only nineteen, and now,
seven years later you are gone,
shot dead in the Colorado coal fields
by a man as brutal as the Turks
who looted and burned our village,
when you were just a boy.

Did you offer yourself as a hostage,
like Daskaloyiannis of Sphakia?
The Turks flayed him alive.
I pray your suffering was less
than his, though you gave no less
than your life for the miners.

Gentle son, who tamed wild creatures,
going about the village showing
your friends how you'd taught
rabbits to play with dogs, birds
to perch on the backs of cats.
Spirit of infinite patience.

In what wild country
did you take your last breath?
Unmarried and childless,
had you died in our village,
we would have dressed you
in a groom's finery, knowing
death would be your only bride.
Did the priest kiss your cold
cheeks and pray that you
be pardoned all your sins?

What sins, I ask?
Your brother read me the letter,
telling of how thousands of men
and women marched silently
behind your funeral coach.
The letter says you died a martyr
for the union cause.

In America they called you Louis Tikas.
I weep, and pray that by now
you have seen the beauty of Paradise.

Back in Wales, I thought my trained voice
would be put to better use than singing
through the bars of an American jail cell.
But indeed, I've gathered crowds
in the alley outside this filthy jail,
where they've thrown me and my two
little girls for my sassing a militiaman.
When he grabbed me by my wrap,
and I fought back, people in the streets
cried "shame," and other words I won't repeat.

I can't see out, but I hear shouts
and cheers, and when I begin to sing,
"The Union Forever," I motion through
the broken window for them to join in.

Soon the men in the other cells are singing
and the crowd is singing, and I think
my voice has never sounded finer,
or ever been put to better use.

"Hoorah, boys, hoorah," we all
sing together and close with screams,
whistles and shouts that linger, echoing,
the very air a grand opera house,
no finery required.

After the police drive everyone away,
I go back to *Rigoletto*, ready to sing
"Cara Nome," until Gilda
takes her dying breath.
I begin, my voice rising
movingly as her life ebbs away.

My young daughters should be afraid,
but instead they sleep, curled together

on a soiled cot, dreaming of clouds
drifting down from the Twin Peaks,
then floating among the white tents
of the Ludlow camp, not remembering
how the militia torched them, until
the whole colony burned to the ground.

I will remember the sight of the flames,
the sound of screams, until my own life
ends, the last note boldly ringing,
just before I take my own
last, coveted breath.

V. AFTERMATH

Life must be lived forward, but it can only be
understood backward.

—Søren Kierkegaard

OUT OF THE DEPTHS

Barron Beshoar writes about his father

A coaldust-stained face and wracking cough,
black lung, pneumonia or a wretched cold,
lingering through the long winter.
High fevers, diarrhea, convulsions.
My father didn't always have a diagnosis,
but his ministrations comforted
and often gave the miners
or their wives or babies
a chance for better health.

He sometimes let me hold
a newborn, with skin warm and soft
as the petal of a flower.
I stroked its little face and silently bade it
leave the mines and live a long life.

Typhus and cholera
my father knew he couldn't
always cure, but he explained
in a tender voice how they mustn't
drink from the filthy cisterns.

As a small boy, I rode with him
along the river, in our Overland
touring car, to see a sick miner
or miner's baby or woman in labor.
After we left our house in Trinidad,
we turned off the headlights
and bumped down a rutted road,
me on the floor, in the dark,
smelling gasoline and axle grease
and listening for the whine of bullets.
Sometimes all I heard was a meadowlark,
singing as if it didn't know
the difference between beauty and pain.

Searchlights skimmed over us,
the mine guards hoping to spot us
and send bullets our way, my father
hated for being the miners' doctor.

Days after Ludlow burned, my father,
mother and I drove through the town,
where miners in red bandanas stood
in sunlight at every corner, holding
Winchesters, and waving at us as we passed,
their hands streaked blue-black, but shining
somehow, as if the coal dust was turning
under the heat of it all, under the pressure,
into a scattering of diamond flecks.

MY FATHER'S STORY

He had black lung, but chewing tobacco's
what killed him, cancer all through his body
before he died, closing his eyes on Easter
morning when the bees were droning
their way from flower to flower, crocus just
up and the first forsythia, yellow as butter.

Not too long before that day, as winter
light dwindled into sunset, each day
softening into spring, when I was on a visit,
his voice came sharp from the recliner,
shaped so perfectly to his body he appeared
to grow there. "Sit down," he ordered,
and I did, perched on the edge of my chair,
watching his lips for another command,
or the beginning of one of the stories
I'd heard a hundred times, about how
he'd once saved a trapper boy
from a runaway coal car, or hidden
his food from the mine rats.

I searched his dark, amphibious face,
chaw rounding out his cheek,
and I listened, caught in his black eyes, hapless
daughter, only child of his old age, myself
motherless, expected to mother him,
watching his lips as they began moving,
telling me again how he carried his only
son— crushed by falling timber—
out of the mine in his arms,

"I've got a story I never told anyone,"
he said, bringing a chill, my spine
electric, the ticking clock weaving a web
of sound. "I didn't listen to the tales,"
he said, "of what my friends saw,

a woman in white, a ghostly procession
of men carrying their pails, bad dreams.
Dreams can come true," he said, stopped
and looked at me before covering his face
with his hand and whispering, "We shouldn't
have worked in the mine that day."

I know he waited for me, his rational daughter
who never worried about spilt salt or black cats,
to tell him it was all superstition, no truth to it
at all, and so, that's what I said, firmly.

No truth to it at all.

I hoped he couldn't see my hands
shaking at the sudden memory
of my brother's face, fixed in a grimace,
as if he had indeed seen something
unspeakable before dying.

APRIL 20, 1934

Pearl Jolly remembers Louis Tikas

Rain in the air a ways off, smell of smoke,
a baby's cry, sharp, easing into sobs,
then echoing, carried by the wind.
Twenty years ago in Colorado,
I was a miner's wife, miner's lover
and miner's daughter, born
in a CF & I shack, and here
in dreary Rock Springs,
far from those days, that place,
I'm still a miner's wife, still Pearl,
a miner's daughter, my father's jewel,
my mother's lovely hope given a name.

When my husband left the Colorado
fields during the strike, left me alone
in our colony tent, I took a lover
who taught me words in Greek
I still remember but won't
ever say, lest by speaking them
they'll fly away forever, like birds,
bound for the moon or stars
or other places I'll never go.
I think these words in Louie's voice—
hero and martyr—and he is with me
again, and we are dancing, young
and alive, our steps in unison,
the music flowing through us
as the sky turns the color
of smoke and blood.

DOLLS

My hope chest holds a box
of little dolls my brother Jimmy
carved from scraps of piñon
when he was a trapper boy
in the Tabasco pit, working
under a headlamp,whittling
to who knows what tune
in his young head, doll
after doll, if you could call
them that, thick bodies, topped
by fierce faces, no two alike
but each a creature amazingly alive
with pain, hunger, or fear.

Who could have thought
a boy of ten could dream up
such frightening expressions?
I know I'm seeing into the dark
hours of Jimmy's life back then,
feeling the urgent, careful knife
strokes taking up the hours,
the loneliness.

What possesses me to say
a tragic early death befell him?
No, he grew up, survived the Primero
blast and struck at Ludlow
with our father.
Door boy to miner, he progressed
from boy to man, and he works there
still with his own sons.
"Work," he says, "is work."

In '37, I drove from Denver
for a visit, and asked him
if he remembered the dolls

he carved with no more light
than a headlamp spared.
He coughed into a cloth
and gathered himself up
until his chest swelled
with an unseemly laugh.
"Can't believe you kept
them little chips of wood.
They was no more than kindling.
Toss them into the fire.
They were meant
to burn long ago."

MARY PETRUCCI DREAMS OF HER CHILDREN

Months passed before I slept the night, years
passed before I slept without nightmares, and
then each night passed blankly as a little death.
You can read about me, poor Mary,
who lost all her babies in the pit,
the cellar dug to save us that became a grave.
Poor Mary, who nearly lost her mind from grief.
I woke up in hell, my children cold beside me,
when hours before the iron cover over us
had been too hot to touch.

How long did I sit among the dead?—
my own, Lucy, two and a half, Frank,
six months, and Joe, my oldest, nearly five.
My friend Cedi died and her girl Lucy,
and her boy Onafrio.
Patria Valdez died, with her children
Eulala, Mary, Elvira, and Rudolf.
Cloriva and Rodgerio Pedregone, also children,
died, all smothered under tent number fifty-eight,
lying before me that morning, the children
clasped in one another's arms,
the two women lying over them.

I tore my way up and out into first light,
the colony still burning, everything
not metal or buried, reduced to ash,
or smoldering heaps of charcoal—
stoves, bedsteads, bedding, pots, pans,
buckets, cups, tools, toys, clothes.
I'd emerged from the cellar to see
the end of the world, but only my world
had truly ended, my life as a mother.
Many years later I saw them in a dream—
my Lucy, Frank and Joe, sister and brothers
in death, they occupied no heaven,

they were no longer children, they spoke
in grave full sentences—each word shaped
from silver and twilight—their eyes
open as they floated freely
through everlasting space, each
filled with greater knowledge
of eternity than any god.

Dreaming of them in their miraculous
wholeness brought me peace, and my frozen
blood, wild for life, began to warm
and flow once again,
like consecrated water
spilling down a streambed
across bright reaches
of a land I'd yet to see.

Author's Note

Throughout the earliest days of their operation and beyond, Colorado mines were notoriously unsafe. Between 1884 and 1912, 1,708 miners were killed in mining accidents in the state, more than twice the national average. Camps in the Southern Field were located up isolated canyons. Miners lived in ramshackle company houses and bought food, supplies and alcohol at company stores and saloons. Entrances to the "closed" camps were patrolled by armed guards.

The United Mine Workers of America called a strike in 1913 after operators failed to meet seven union demands:

1. Recognition of UMWA as a bargaining agent.
2. A ten percent increase in wages on the tonnage rates.
    (Each miner was paid by the ton of coal he mined, not by the hour.)
3. An eight-hour workday.
4. Payment for "dead work." (Miners were paid only for the coal they mined. Shoring, timbering, and laying track was not paid work.)
5. Union-elected check-weighmen.
6. The right to trade in any store, and choose own doctors and places of residence.
7. Enforcement of and adherence to Colorado mining laws.

Approximately seventy percent of the Las Animas County workforce struck on September 23, 1913. The miners and their families who lived in the camps were immediately evicted and relocated to tent colonies (on land leased and in tents provided by UMWA) located at strategic spots near canyon entrances, in order to intercept strikebreakers.

More than 1,200 miners and their families, a population speaking more than twenty-four different languages, lived in two hundred tents in the Ludlow Colony, the largest of the many colonies organized by UMWA. The coal mine operators were quick to bring in strikebreakers. High-powered searchlights shone over the tents throughout the night and Colorado Fuel and Iron constructed an armored car known as the "Death Special" that periodically sprayed the colonies with machine-gun fire. Violence quickly intensified.

On October 28, Governor Elias Ammons ordered a thousand militia into southern Colorado, to be commanded by Adjutant General John Chase and Lt. Karl Linderfelt, formerly head of CF&I security and mine guards. Over the months that followed, many of the recruits coming to southern Colorado to replace militia leaving active duty were known strikebreakers or Baldwin-Felts thugs and gunmen, brought to Colorado from the east or midwest.

Six months into the strike, Major Patrick Hamrock was named by Governor Ammons to replace Chase. Violence continued to escalate. On the morning of April 20, 1914, most accounts indicate that Karl Linderfelt set off three handcrafted bombs, purportedly a prearranged signal to militia to open fire on the tents. Militiamen, atop Water Tank Hill, began firing a machine gun on the Ludlow Colony. Strikers—some of whom had already taken positions in the canyon—and their wives and children ran from the tents into the arroyo, as the canvas was being shredded by bullet holes, or took refuge in storage cellars beneath the tents.

Toward the end of the day, militiamen ran wildly through the colony, looting and setting fire to the tents. Louis Tikas, the Greek leader of the colony, and James Fyler, the paymaster, were apprehended by the military as they were trying to guide terrified women and children to safety. Tikas was later found with three bullet holes in his back. Fyler had been shot in the head. The next day, as Red Cross volunteers were going through the ruins of the colony, they found two women and eleven children in a cellar beneath an area that had once supported a tent, all asphyxiated.

Despite numerous hearings and investigations (and indictments against 120 strikers and union officials), all members of the National Guard were cleared of any wrongdoing.

Only after the tragedy did John D. Rockefeller claim to recognize "the kinship of humanity"—a lesson learned too late for those who suffered and died in the Colorado mines, and "Colorado Coal Field Wars." Yet, ultimately, as George McGovern notes, it is difficult to delineate heroes and villains precisely. Not all mine guards were thugs, or all coal operators "heartless profiteers," and not all miners and labor leaders were altruistically motivated. Nevertheless, working people everywhere continue to be victimized by the same kind of greed and moral insensibility that lead to the tragic events culminating in what has come to be known as the "Ludlow Massacre."

About the Author

Eleanor Swanson's awards include finalist in the 2001 *Missouri Review* Larry Levis Editors' Prize, a Fellowship from the National Endowment for the Arts, and a Colorado Council on the Arts Fellowship in literature. Her book, *A Thousand Bonds: Marie Curie and the Discovery of Radium,* winner of the 2003 Stevens Manuscript Prize, published by the National Federation of State Poetry Societies, was a finalist in poetry for the 2004 Colorado Book Award. She teaches at Regis University in Denver.

Sources

Adams, Graham. *The Age of Industrial Violence, 1910-1915: The Activities and Findings of the U.S. Commission on Industrial Relations.* New York: Columbia University Press, 1966

Baker-Hauck, Chelsey. "Massacre at Ludlow," *University of Denver Magazine*, January 2003.

Barrans, Richard E, Jr. "Coal to Diamonds," 11 July 2003. http://newton.dep.anl.gov/askasci/chem00/chem00349/htm>.

Beshoar, Barron B. *Out of the Depths: The Story of John R. Lawson, a Labor Leader.* Denver: Golden Bell Press, 1942.

Caputo, Silvio J., Jr,. *The Death of Spring.* Port Washington, NY: Ashley Books, Inc., 1984.

Colorado Coal Field War Project. 14 November 2003 <www.cdheritage.org/heritage/ludlow/cfhist2.html>.

Donachy, Patrick L. *A Rendezvous with Shame.* Trinidad, CO: The Inkwell, 1989.

—. United We Stand: UMWA Women's Auxiliary, Local 9856. Trinidad, CO: The Inkwell, 1990.

Ellison, Todd. Nomad *Private Railroad Car Scrapbook.* 15 May 2003 <http://swcenter.fortlewis.edu/inventory/RGSNomad.htm>.

Gitelman, Howard M. *Legacy of the Ludlow Massacre: A Chapter in American Labor Relations.* Philadelphia: University of Philadelphia Press, 1988.

Korson, George. *Coal Dust on the Fiddle: Songs and Stories of the Bituminous Industry.* Philadelphia: University of Philadelphia Press, 1943.

Long, Priscilla. *Where the Sun Never Shines: A History of America's Bloody Coal6 Industry*. New York: Paragon House, 1989.
Margolis, Eric. "Mining Photographs: Unearthing the Meaning of Historical Photos." Radical History Review, 4033-49, 1988.

McGovern, George and Leonard F. Guttridge. *The Great Coalfield War*. Boulder: University Press of Colorado, 1996.

O'Neal, Mary Thomas. *Those Damn Foreigners*. Hollywood, CA: Minerva, 1971.

Papanikolas, Zeese. *Buried Unsung: Louis Tikas and the Ludlow Massacre*. Salt Lake City: University of Utah Press, 1982.

Sunseri, Alvin R. *The Ludlow Massacre: A Study in the mis-employment of the National Guard*. Waterloo, Iowa: Salvadore Books, 1972

Zinn, Howard, Dana Frank and Robin D.G. Kelley. *Three Strikes: Miners, Musicians, Salesgirls, and the Fighting Spirit of Labor's Last Century*. Boston: Beacon Press, 2001.

Printed in the United States
53075LVS00007B/211-312

9 780977 803460